The Journey Home to

Abba

Camella Rose Mac Donald

WESTBOW
PRESS®
A DIVISION OF THOMAS NELSON
& ZONDERVAN

Interior Graphics/Art Credit to Patty Maher on Title Page.

WestBow Press books may be ordered through booksellers or by contacting:

WestBow Press
A Division of Thomas Nelson & Zondervan
1663 Liberty Drive
Bloomington, IN 47403
www.westbowpress.com
1 (866) 928-1240

ISBN: 978-1-4908-8665-7 (sc)
ISBN: 978-1-4908-8666-4 (e)

Library of Congress Control Number: 2015910519

Print information available on the last page.

WestBow Press rev. date: 07/23/2015

This poetry book is a gift to the Father, Son and Holy Spirit who have been my everything. I give all glory and honor to Jesus Christ my Savior who is truly a friend who sticks closer than any brother. I give glory to the Holy Spirit who was truly the ghostwriter of this poetry and everything I have written or will ever write. I give glory to the Father for truly being my Abba and understanding how important it is to me that He is my Abba. I love Jesus and am thankful that He chose to save me and my 4 children. All honor and glory and praise to the Father, Son and Holy Spirit.

"He led them forth by the right way"

Psalm 107:7 Changeful experience often leads the anxious believer to enquire "Why is it thus with me?" I looked for light, but lo, darkness came; for peace, but behold trouble. I said in my heart, my mountain standeth firm, I shall never be moved. Lord, thou dost hide Thy face, and I am troubled. It was but yesterday that I could read my title clear; to-day my evidences are bedimmed, and my hopes are clouded. Yesterday I could climb to Pisgah's top, and view the landscape o'er, and rejoice with confidence in my future inheritance; to-day, my spirit has no hopes, but many fears; no joys, but much distress. Is this part of God's plan with me? Can this be the way in which God would bring me to heaven? Yes, it is even so. The eclipse of your faith, the darkness of your mind, the fainting of your hope, all these things are but parts of God's method of making you ripe for the great inheritance upon which you shall soon enter. These trials are for the testing and strengthening of your faith-they are waves that wash you further upon the rock-they are winds which waft your ship the more swiftly towards the desired haven. According to David's words, so it might be said of you, "so He bringeth them to their desired haven." By honor and dishonor, by evil report and by good report, by plenty and by poverty, by joy and by distress, by persecution and by peace, by all these things is the life of your souls maintained, and by each of these are you helped on your way. Oh, think not, believer, that your sorrows are out of God's plan; they are necessary parts of it. "We must, through much tribulation, enter the kingdom." Learn, then, even to "count it all joy when ye fall into divers temptations."

"O let my trembling soul be still,

And wait Thy wise, Thy holy will!

I cannot, Lord, Thy purpose see,

Yet all is well since ruled by Thee."

Look and Live

Desires of the flesh, or the things we touch, feel and taste. Things such as these are passing away. When we leave our earthly tent behind so will the desires which were attached to the flesh. We cannot bring our desires and longings with us at all. So, then what should we set our eyes upon? We should set our eyes on Jesus Christ who is the Author and Finisher of this great faith and on the calling He has given to each of us before the foundation of the earth. We must always keep our eyes steadfast on the mark to complete the work of the high calling in this Great Commission of soul winning. For only the heathen should worry about what they should wear, drink and eat. We as Christians are fully aware that we serve a good and faithful Master. So we should seek Him and not gratify the lusts of the flesh. Anything attached to our flesh brings death. We must look and live which means that even as Moses lifted up the serpent in the wilderness and people looked and lived, we too should look and live as we look to the cross. We need daily to give up our earthly treasure which will soon fade and look to Christ Jesus to gratify our needs. We must ever be mindful of our heavenly home and store up treasures there. The spiritual world is more real than this physical world will ever be. Our physical dwelling will one day end and our spiritual world will last throughout eternity. Let's consider the outcome of looking to Jesus and living for Him in this lifetime. The reward out weighs anything this world can ever offer. Just to hear the Father say "thou good and faithful servant" and to enter into an eternal home with the blessed trinity will be worth giving up anything and everything this world can offer.

What is it that causes us to give in to our desires and lusts of the flesh? It is the fear that overtakes our faith and causes us to waiver like a ship in a storm. We are tossed back and forth until fear overtakes us and we give in to our desires thinking that it will bring rest for our souls. Fear is a paralyzing emotion. However, perfect Love casts out all fear. When perfect Love enters there is no room for fear. What better place to meet perfect Love then in the House of God. I went in with a burden and a prayer and came out with peace and His perfect Love. I went to the alter for prayer and the Almighty met me there with His arms outstretched in Perfect Love. He held me like a father holds his small child enveloped in His everlasting arms. He took away the fears of the dark and I knew everything was going to be alright. I felt Him once before as I cried out for Him to hug me and hold me near to His bosom. Like a blanket at night covers a child so His blanket covered me. I told Him never to go. I wanted His presence forever. It's been a while. But tonight I felt Him once again. Someone spoke, "God is hugging you and holding you in His arms." I knew it was Him because He hears every prayer and His peace once again enveloped me." I just want to praise Him to whoever reads this. He sees each tear that falls and He knows our every fear and flaw. He cares for us because we are His dear children and He wants us to look and live. We must only believe. He is the same yesterday, today and forever more. The things of this world can never satisfy and Jesus is ever calling you through all your running and chasing after your desires to fulfill you. All that is really needed to fill the empty soul is Jesus who can meet every need and fill every empty hurting soul with His Love.

Brokenness

What does it mean to be broken?

The dreams once enlightened...have passed

visions of tomorrow have long been

dimmed,

into a lethargic sense.

emptiness…

trails along life's journey

which once lead,

to hopes and aspirations,

have passed into roads

uncertain,

twists and turns along the way,

have led to windows,

clouded by mist which

cannot be…

wiped clear to see that

vision,

predestined before the earth

was formed,

forks in the road, thwart truth…

the destination…

there below... waters so deep,

seek to envelope

into depths of despondency,

brokenness… dark paths… deep

waters…

windows that cannot be shattered,

endlessly one bangs against the pane,

lights a candle in the night,

fights the currents which rage,

against the soul,

once again.... despair…

that's what it means to be broken.

This is for all that are going through a dark hour of the soul. Remember, that joy comes in the morning and through the mourning Jesus will shine His brightest. All must come through trials and tribulations they are inescapable. Mostly all of the people in the bible have experienced such things. However, they were more than overcomers and God used them to do great things for His great purpose and glory,

Misunderstood

How does it feel when you're misunderstood and no-one understands the circumstances that have brought you to this place and time?

How does it feel when you have searched and found that nothing is what it seems?

How does it feel when you trust only to be forsaken?

How does it feel when you reach out in hopes of comfort and you are ill-treated?

How does it feel when the words you have spoken in love have been misevaluated?

How does it feel when you try to please someone and they turn away and are not at all pleased?

How does it feel to be misunderstood when you know that you love God with all of your heart and no-one believes you?

How does it feel when you are so desperate for just a crumb from the table of love and you are shunned?

How does one think it feels to be misunderstood?

Feelings

feelings, unstable,

emotions, the ride,

up, down, side to side,

moods come, they go,

your left...feeling,

lost... uneasy...

the flesh...the voice...

the lie...TRUTH...FACT IS...

the CROSS....CALVARY...

feelings? NO… emotions? NO…

but...the Word. The Sword.

the SPIRIT... fights circumstance...

gives vision...purpose...VICTORY to

OVERCOME …

Angel of Light

When the devil comes as an angel of light,

do you stand or do you take flight,

when he comes with a smile and a glare,

will you sense that it might be a snare,

do you give in or attest to the plight,

of the angel of light assigned for you,

When he says this is good and it will bring

you life,

do you agree and give in to the plight…

that was never the light,

does he entice and bring false hope,

visions of rapture that never do come.

for when you say yes… the darkness is there,

and you see the shadow taking over the light,

that never was there but the cunnings of him,

with the smile and the glare,

whose real desire,

was to capture you unaware.

raise up your sword when he does come in,

for it's never too late to fight the good fight,

the weapons he has are imposters of Him,

he uses the Word to lure and deceive,

we use God's Word and he shall retrieve,

raise up the verse take off his cloak…

expose his true side and do not give in,

for the weapons we use take a thousand to flight,

the father of lies is put to shame,

and the angel once radiant,

is thrown to the flame

NO WEAPON FORMED AGAINST US SHALL PROSPER!!!!!

One Last Time

One last time He spoke...

one last time....

I forgive I forget...

but one last time...

yes... my child, you are mine...

time after time...

till the ending of days.

A Father, who loves,

must chastise the one,

who continues to go astray...

He warned and He guided but...

His child disobeyed... over and over

again... It grieved Him so to watch

the fall... and it hurt Him to see..

the mistake... and a lesson... never learned...

many a time He opened His arms and such comfort

He did give... yet over and over,

time went on... His child never did grow,

so out of His love... discipline came...

as He spoke... with tears... that's the "last time"

and such growth did appear in that child of His...

with arms lifted high His child did say, "I truly do surrender"....

and great peace was received...and God's grace came again...

As He embraced His child...death went away and true life began.

All through the love of the FATHER

Pleasure is for a moment and consequences are for a lifetime. Each time we are exposed to temptation we must think and rethink who it will affect in the long run. Many times it not only affects us but the next generation. With that in mind let us seek wisdom in every choice we make. Sexual sins are damaging not only to ourselves but to those we share them with.

The Altar of Surrender

I went to the alter today.

no-one was there to pray,

I saw the bread, the wine,

knew it was just HIM and I,

alone face to face,

i poured out my all,

i cried I surrender, I surrender

ALL,

Wasn't sure if He heard me nor understood,

my beckon call,

it was at that moment,

silence fell within my mind and heart,

I ate the bread, drank the wine,

it's been some time,

silence broke.... my veil was torn

from me...

it was then,

a reply…... the music played,

no-one knew ....it was just Him and I,

and the melody.." I surrender all to you,

all to you"... and then i knew,

He understood, the condition

of my heart, and He took it all,

now anew at the alter

just Him and I

I Cried Yes

I sat beside the pool today;

He said "Do you want to be well?"

I cried ....YES

as tears ran down my face,

i felt the need to rise,

it's been years… No change,

something within brought me

to the pool each day,

wanting to get in,

healing waters stirred,

my heart grew more disturbed

as others walked away...free…

I still waiting at the pool…

grew anxious,

until one day I thought to move…

and actively respond…

"Do you want to be well?"

"YES LORD" "THEN PICK UP YOUR MAT" said HE,

it was then healing waters flowed,

within not without...as I began to rise,

i felt him touch my wounds, I was well

I began to walk... then shout...then scream...

I am free!!! I am Free!!! It wasn't the pool at

Bethesda, it was HE!!!

Dark is the Night

dark is the night that holds us

at times captive to our imaginings

dark moments hours of the soul

which keep us bound to our

circumstance

our life

our fears of tomorrow

which never come to pass

it's only in our mind

that we think.. we are…

as a shadow of the life which follows..

that haunts us at times…

we dread our next moment…

the lies… the enemy…

of our soul…has a grip so tight..

dare we try to escape….dark…

the anguish… as we walk through the cave,…

alone at times…searching…searching….

for the light… a glimpse of daybreak…

is our only blessed assurance

at intervals we see the dim light

trying to rescue us from the darkness that…

tries so hard to overtake us.

at moments the light intrigues us

at times compels us to…

follow it into hope..

at moments we do and find that the light is good and there is hope to get out…

darkness gone… light surrounds us and truth prevails… we are free…

Trust in the Lord

Trust in the lord with all of your heart.

do not stray to the right or to the left

stand firm and know that He is there in every circumstance of life

trust Him like no other.

He is our dearest friend

acknowledge Him in all your ways

in the rising and the laying down

seek Him with all of your heart and He shall direct your paths

Paths of righteousness He shall direct you to.

Fear not for The Lord is with you wherever you may go.

In the darkest of nights in the deepest of trials His hand reaches out for you to take hold of

He whispers in your ear in a still small voice

"I am with you".

He sees every tear that falls and He holds them in a flask

Trust HIM!!

The Roaring Lion

he comes like a roaring lion

the enemy of our soul,

God says laugh with joy,

for the adversary has no hold,

he is underfoot and he has no ground

to stand he cannot…

fall he shall with the witness we own…

the testimony of our lives and the word

of God takes ten thousand to flight,

what does the foe have on us,

his destiny is hell,

and ours eternal life,

the roaring lion let him roar,

for we have the sword,

and God himself whose Son is

the KING OF KINGS and LORD OF LORDS

The GREAT LION OF JUDAH, and when he roars the earth shall tremble and the rocks give way as the enemy takes his position under the feet of the mighty lion of JUDAH. All hail the lion of the tribe of JUDAH HAA HAAA HEE HEE HEE to the lion who has no roar the defeated foe under the feet of JESUS the MIGHTY LION OF JUDAH

Trust

Trust is a word no-one can fathom

Trust is a word no-one can touch

So far, so far, so far out there

Once you felt…

Emotions…

The capability…

To feel…

to know

And be known

Trust…

a thought…

a moment…

I've never really come

To know…

Is it out there?

Or is there anybody

Out there?

What is trust?

A thought..

A feeling perhaps…

Who knows?

Have you seen it?

Witnessed it?

Been in touch with it?

Felt it?

Been captivated by the

Illusion of it?

Tell me…tell me…

What is it?

I've never known…

Never felt…

Never experienced…

Such a word…

Trust…

I am not sure if that word

Has substance…

Existence..

Or anything that can be fact…

Let it be known…

If there is a human

That you dare to try it

With…

I have only met one that I could truly trust. His name is Jesus Christ. Not mother nor father, neither sister nor brother and not even a husband can behold such trust. It is only Jesus Christ and Him alone will I ever trust.

How to Get Happy

True happiness comes about when we let go of our view of what brings happiness. Let go of the idea of getting happiness through a mate, finances, or anything that you think will bring you happiness. In fact when we Love God first and foremost it is then we begin to become truly happy or joyful or glad or any word that you would like to put there. Because our search for happiness and joy is really a longing for God. When that longing is filled by God and God alone then and only then will we finally feel the joy that we long for. Depressed people are really depressed because they have their idea of getting happiness a little backwards. Negativity brings depression. However, when we seek God with all of our hearts our thinking will change as we are renewed by His word and His love. In fact one could actually love their mate a whole lot more if one does not make that love an idol but seek after God first. It is then that one could truly flourish in that love and truly love that person and be loved by that person with great love and joy. I got all this excitement from reading C.S. Lewis's life of depression and introverted life before His encounter with God and how he came out when he found that God was His source of great joy and he then became an extrovert with many friends and a blessed life. God bless all that read this and my desire is that many will be changed by this and know that there is hope for every despondent soul. Look up God is waiting to give you His love and great joy.

The Signet Ring

My king gave me His signet ring

said I could use His name,

see, I am His bride and He gave

me the authority,

He gave me His Word that I could use

this power to speak in His name

He gave me His ring as proof of His love

you cannot see it but I wear it with pride,

He is my husband and I am His bride,

He defends me like no other, He is the lover

of my soul, see He has given me His ring

and He will never divorce me,

He loves me so

I have His signet ring,

proof of His love today

and a sign forever of His love to me

I wear His signet ring

the lover of my soul…

Pawn

you feel like a pawn

in the hands of an enemy

he watches your every move

and he challenges you

at every turn

you think

you feel

you back off

he tries to win

to take you captive

your mind

twists…screams

emotions stagger

confused to which

way to go

left…right…

he pushes you to do…

hesitate indeed…

sometimes not sure

the steps are not yours

at times stammered by drives

driven by the force of him

in whose hands you are the pawn

in which he has trapped your thoughts

to his and you are not your own

but driven by his hand that does

not let go of who you are

yet… you know

that anointing is breaking

a power and you will not

be a part of the game

that he plays…for the voice

of a Mightier Master has taken over

and is molding as clay… and you are…

now in his Hand and He is moving

and directing…the other hand is

driven away and gone as you yield and wait

to be moved by the Almighty

what once held you captive

no longer will

a person… a mere man

will be shamed

as he watches you

undaunted by his voice

that once bound your inner soul

suddenly has no power

the only force that moves you

is His…and He alone directs

your course…

and guides you

with His eye

no-one will hold

you captive

for what has bound you

has now been loosed

by the power of His Name

he alone prepares the way

the voice of a stranger

you shall not follow

No longer a pawn!! You are loved and guided by the Master!! Emotional bondage and soul ties are broken in the Name of Jesus Christ. Woman though art loosed.

My Heart knows What's Right

my heart knows what's right

and my soul knows better,

my flesh travels to another

place… outside the real me

my mind directs me to truth,

my spirit cries out;

LISTEN.

A small voice whispers don't

stray,

a force outside of me

leads another way,

yet… my heart knows what's right

the Lord is near, and longs to

end my struggle

but won't intervene for there is

a better way,

angels watch on awaiting victory,

to an endless battle within me,

struggles rage and lions roar,

as my wrists bare the chains,

that have me bound to a lie… a choice…my own demise…

yet… my deepest depths knows better

as my soul cries out,

for victory's plea and a banner

of surrender

I stand and stand, ignoring each lie,

as it fights against my being,

my heart knows what's right… as my spirit leads me on,

to a truth that is realer than anything I've known,

a reality… the still small voice… the Spirit of

the Lord,

is the Key to my heart, soul and mind,

freedom to do what is right,

Temptation

when temptation comes

run

when it lures

flee

when it entices

rebuke it

when it nears

God will make

a way

in its midst

run for the hills

run to the valley

run into His arms

speak... shout

the Word...

resist evil

the blood prevails

protects..delivers

Fighting the Good Fight

We have all authority to fight the good fight of faith. When the enemy comes in cast Him out. When you feel you are making lead way take guard. When we press in the forces of hell will fight with all of their might to trip us up. We have the authority to cast them down and we must use it or we shall not be overcomers. God has done the amazing and transformed that which the devil meant for evil. However, God is so great that He is using it for good. The same temptation has come into my life time and time again. God has shown me that only I could take authority over it and cast it out for good. He gave us His Son's name to use against all the powers of hell and I am determined to fight and use that glorious name now and let the fires of hell be swallowed up in victory. Use His Name.

Lies

lies spoken over you...

from a voice of one known...

your ears hear as it enters

your heart... and you feel the sting

that bites at your flesh,

as it gnaws at your bones,

as you waste away,

from the bitterness of it all,

one way to be free of it,

is to capture the murmur,

the whisper of the voice that

desires to destroy that which

is yours... your hope... your destiny...

a future filled with truth empowered by

vision, inspired by wisdom and given

as a gift to you

The Mask

underneath the mask… a scar…

no-one views… never seen.

everyone wears one… many forms

of personality

where are you when you hide

behind your covering?

why is your soul so shattered

the face once so bright with joy

what made you paint the mask…

of many forms and shades of feelings?

transforming identity into non reality

take off your mask

expose the mark that

cast you down…

deep within your heart

the unseen stain… the secret scar

the lie that binds you

to your past

strip off the mask… the covering…

lay it down… beneath

the feet… beneath the tree…

under the blood…the sacrifice…

Calvary,

If I could Change the Past

If I could change the past,

change the hearts of those

I tried to touch,

if I could have looked and lived

even more to Christ

to renew their minds

by the love within me,

which is in Him that compels

all to come

to the banquet table

God can Speak

can God speak when no voice can be heard

can He speak when no word can be uttered?

though the wind blow and the rain fall

His voice is but a whisper

still and small in the depths of your heart

He taps at your door

bid Him to enter

the journey home at times confusing

distant callings ring unsettling

you find yourself searching for something

emotions and yearnings for the hope of

tomorrow

leaves you wondering if God knows your questions

doubts and fears of what could be

has you searching for answers from the voice…

OF GOD…

though He shows you His Word and things once

so clear…

are complex and not reassuring…

you ponder if the voice once so strong

and confirming…

was really the voice

of the Master you serve…

Each Step We Take

each step we take… directed by Him

He holds the future in His hand

each path we choose… directed by Him

a solid foundation… here we stand

no tempest storm nor trial deep

can keep us from the ultimate plan

though we strive…to know that will

each day is in His hand…

no depth… no power… nor fowlers snare…

can thwart the destined path we travel

each step we take… directed by Him,

He holds the future in His hand

A poem for My King

I'm writing a poem to my King,

My Master my everything,

He's the ruler of my heart,

My desire… panting after Him,

He loves me and His delight

Is in my praises,

I dance before Him in the presence

Of His angelic host,

Bowing before Him with admiration

I give Him glory for He is my Lord,

My King…Master of everything,

My thoughts of pleasure,

For His joy over me draws me into

Writing a poem to my King

Delight Thyself in the Lord

if thou delight thyself in the Lord

than we can forever stand

and never fall

when the tempest come

to cast a load of sin

we can trust that God

will carry the yoke

the burden no other can

take

He alone… stands at Zion's door

He beckons enter in

when sin takes over…

and convictions grow weak…

that once burned strong…

lingering by the wayside

your heart breaks

yet He is still forever strong

calling from His sanctuary

the voice of the Lord says

Come… Trust… Behold…Victory's glory…

awaits you as you rise up

standing firm

a banner over head held high

for the chosen Anointed One…

He the lifter of your head,

draws nigh,

for He hears your every call

every tear is in His flask

as He pours His oil over you

with joy you shall enter in…

distress forever gone

the banner… His protection…

His great love…

Your shield…

forever over you in love…

delights in your reaching…

God of a Second Chance

my God ...the God of mercy...

Calling for us... He waits,

ever waiting, watching for the

return

calling... waiting,

time after time... we fall

He helps us

still we trip

never shuns us...

the God of second

chances...

David, Saul, Moses and such

turned around

falls behind

glory ahead

first time lost

second chance

grace abounds

all the more

we pant for Him

as He too awaits

our arrival

to give the Mission…

Accomplished…

The second chance

His View

Our victory…

HIS GLORY

He Lights My Candle in the Night (Psalm 18)

He draws me out of many waters

as calamity

attempts to flood

my world

I called upon the Lord

and His ear did hearken to

my cry

as my pleadings ever went

before Him

then He bowed the heavens

came down with darkness under

His feet...

He drew back the oppression

and set me upon a high mountain

because He did delight in me

for thou will light my candle

and He will enlighten my

darkness

the night will turn back

and day will break

with joy coming forth

as the candle burns on

The Light... My Light...

burning in the night...

The Invisible Hand of God

the invisible hand of God

has touched you,

in ways you thought,

uncertain,

you have felt His hand

in ways unknown

bringing you to that place

in which His

voice is heard

He calls for you,

beckons you to come…

He longs to fill the darkness

lonely places of the heart

woes and valleys deep…

waters overflowing …

with streams of tears and

fears you alone can't

face…

He beckons come…

for He lights a candle

just for you

snares and coils

round about

confusions heightened

by distractions

along

the journey

try to steal

from the

anointed one…

chosen by God

to be the voice

of destiny,

for those who

lost their way

God is here,

the dark clouds

under His feet…

He shoots His

arrows…

enemies are

scattered…

days... disasters...

The Lord... Your Lord

is your support...

Come... He is

here,

rest awhile

from your journey

you must be tired

from the load

of cares...

His burden is light

His yoke... so easy,

Come;

Enter... the Holy of Holies

with His embrace,

(Inspired by God through prayer and fasting)

Coming Home Again

coming home again,

it's been awhile,

since I've been there,

near to you and feeling

you close by,

had moments where,

I was soo ready,

to be where you are,

seeking from a distance,

the world out there...

kept me from,

the dwelling place,

my safe abode,

music captivated,

entrances to my

mind.

were closed,

the dance outside,

so different,

enticed my flesh,

to another rhythm,

another beat,

only the world

could know,

drew me,

taken from my

residence,

prisoner of another

spirit…

some other dwelling

not my own,

never felt right,

just a temporary

fix,

for the void,

NOW…

I'm missing home…

where my Father is…

Calling for me…

it's been awhile,

I think I'll take

the journey,

He awaits,

I know,

my coming home

Changes

Changes..

prayer changes

life… meaning… destination…

Changes the soul

depths… conscious

awareness of

the inner man…

wanting to be…

different..

the Spirit

convictions grab

the you…

that you

hold on to…

clinging…

ever tighter,

to that man…

so dead…

alive… is Christ,

ever in you…

helping… wooing

drawing the new

creation to

the better

way…

you release…

let go…

what joy…

freedom

at last…

you've arrived…

rest…

Let the Fire Burn

let the fire burn…

set ablaze

the world around

us

may it surround,

move… engulf our being

may the power

fall…

endue… enlighten…

burn…

within… without

all about…

move ahead

as the fire

led…

from Egypt

to Canaan

freedom…

strengthens…

let it burn,

desire…

passion,

for the Word

power…

refreshing

boldness,

to speak…

heal,

deliver,

set free…

those dead

in sin…

Let the fire

burn for

them…

to enter…

let the fire

burn…

Pentecost…

tongues,

prophecy,

LOVE,

Let the fire burn

Where the Wind Blows

where the wind blows

there the secret lies,

underneath the wings

as the eagle flies,

He lifts us up,

where no-one knows,

He lays us in,

the cleft of the rock,

on mountain high,

where the wind blows,

no beast dare,

to tarry there,

where the wind blows,

an the eagle flies,

we shall mount up,

within his wings,

there we fly,

above the storm,

beyond the clouds,

into the Spirit,

of our dear rest,

where the wind blows

His presence is,

Blessed Holiness

The Canal

through the canal,

seems so close,

I could almost see,

a hand reaching,

to take me through,

to the other side,

obstacles squeeze,

to prevent the

flow of oxygen,

I struggle,

for the final thrust,

to freedom,

ride the wave,

I can push,

away the pain,

as I grab the hand,

that reaches for me,

I extend mine and hope,

comes alive,

as my head births forth,

to new life,

in Jesus Christ,

I enter His world,

and leave the old,

behind,

joy at last,

the end of

the canal...

Curse

for every curse

there is a blessing,

under the blood,

is the answer,

the serpent's lie,

breathes out death,

life is there,

nearer the cross,

destroys the words,

once ill spoken,

breaks the power

within the soul,

frees the mind,

to know the way,

in our hearts,

on our lips,

the precious Word

of God,

breaks the curse

sets us free,

delivers us from

all temptation,

we are blessed,

and redeemed,

All Hail King Jesus

from whom all blessings

flow…

The Deepest Vault

there within the deepest vault,

He came to break the chains,

which held the deepest,

depths of you,

bound,

He opened many

others,

this one you

kept,

within the boundaries,

of a time,

so far gone,

not even you,

could reach,

to open the

deepest vault,

capsulated…

left

unreached,

so retained,

within your mind,

your soul cried,

mercy..

the chains... the locks...

so tight the seal,

no-one dare to try,

you couldn't even reach,

within yourself,

to be loosed,

or rescued from the

vault... so dark within

the precepts of you,

your mind... soul,... heart...

protected the most inner

part,

that is there within the

vault,

the deepest vault,

Jesus is there...

now He enters...

removes the chains,

the locks,

that which held you,

bondage,

to that pain,

is gone,

He fills it,

and it is clean,

He makes His abode there..

you are whole...

The Anointing

the Anointing is waiting for you,

in that quiet place,

to call upon Him,

to rest upon you,

He wants you to pray,

He wants you to say,

I will give my all

He wants to fill you,

as He did Paul,

on that road blinded,

by the light,

let the fire burn,

let it fall ever upon,

your heart,

your very being,

COME...

enter the Holy Of Holies,

bend your knee,

bow your head,

fall prostrate,

before your Lord,

He is longing…

for you,

let the oil

pour,

upon your head

let the fire burn

in His presence,

feel the Lord,

His power comes,

and stirs,

you are His hands,

you are His feet,

the voice…

mouthpiece…

Sing praise,

As David,

His anointing… falls on you

The Road Less Traveled

so many roads,

forks along the way,

some are rough,

many rocky,

those the roads

less traveled,

others steep,

can hardly climb,

thorns that prick,

the road so narrow,

the strain,

pain along the way,

much rather take the

easy road,

smooth and flat,

with pretty flowers,

wide enough, for

many travelers,

so many people along

this path,

who would want...

the road less traveled,

the road is mapped,

leads them on,

and they follow,

it's easy...

along the worldly

trail.

the red flags...

mark the way,

by the Master...

on this wide trail,

deceiving spirits lead,

them on,

the road most

traveled,

so wide and broad,

lined with lies

all along the

journey,

feels so good,

why change the course,

Yet… up ahead

the path is closing,

for the night approaches,

and dark is the end,

should have chose the

road less traveled,

to bring them

Home to

the Father…

Can't Understand

can't understand with my back

against the wall,

defenses shooting out

of me,

I just can't understand,

the why's and how's and where's

and such,

why I feel the way I do,

I try so hard to explain

myself,

yet never understood,

search for ways to be more clear,

yet the others view…

so tainted…

imageries so saturated

distortions paint his mind

so here I stand,

my back against

the wall,

here unprotected…

with my hands pinned back,

way beyond my heart...

fighting doubts within my mind,

from lies that feed his

thoughts,

powers from who knows where,

threaten the deepest part

of me,

he calls my every word,

fashions as he

pleases,

using his authority,

I can only bow my head,

helplessly against the

wall...

I try so,

to escape the thoughts,

I can't understand...

Change Can Happen

when one wants to change,

it can happen,

no-one knows,

but the one,

when the heart is

in that condition,

it is ready,

to be led,

through the

storm,

no fear of the night,

shall follow,

her view is on…

what's ahead,

for the mind is

fixed and it's

steadfast,

on getting there

at last,

others might not

understand,

for only she

knows the condition,

of her heart,

and wants to follow

the plan,

predestined by God

to follow,

she is so desperate,

to find the path,

that leads on to

the turning,

of her heart,

to the hand

of the Master

The Heart

the heart is so terribly wicked,

who can know it but the Lord,

when thoughts come and we yield,

to the voice of the stranger,

you know he has a plan

to rob you of your walk,

and the good things God

has in store for those

who follow Him,

the thief comes to kill

steal and destroy,

the Lord has come to

give you life,

yield to Him,

His voice will lead

the way,

to blessing and all

good things,

if you happen to give in

to the lie..

the voice of another,

pray..

God can make a way,

put down your ways,

imaginations from the other,

cast your plans upon the altar,

and God will remove mountains,

an enemy has put in your

midst,

the heart will feel the passion,

the mind yielded to the truth,

will leap over a tower,

the voice of the Shepard…

will lead you on,

through your heart's cry,

desire shall burn in you,

for that which is God's will,

He prepares a table for you

in the midst of your enemies,

He fills your heart with gladness,

and His oil flows over you,

as you give Him yourself,

in complete surrender to

His purpose

the heart most seemingly wicked,

can be fashioned into,

a total heart for God,

and His divine purpose,

predestined by Him,

the heart… your heart

give it to Him

to beat with His heart…

Oh Backslider

give me your hearts,

and render not your garments,

come unto me with a pure life,

and I will give you hope

in a dry parched land,

I will walk with you

in the day,

and carry you through

the night,

only give me your heart,

talk with me along your

journey,

and there will

be rest...

along the road

in which

you travel,

I will heal you,

Ohhh come...

dear backslider,

I will love you

freely... (Hosea 14:4)

in your dry parched land.

blossom… blossom like the lily(v.5)

and I will speak to you

in the cool of the day,

I will be your light,

dear traveler in your

darkest hour,

you shall not trip

or fall along the

way,

take words with you..

return… return,

unto your Lord,

He will ransom you

from the serpent's bite

and deliver

you from death's call,

give you LIFE

Call… call upon Him,

He waits for you,

He waits for you,

Ohhh backslider,

The Lord says come!!

won't you come

taste and see that the

Lord is good…

Hosea 14 The Lord our Lord loves you oh backslider and is longing for you in the dry parched land. Will you answer the call? I say oh yes sweet, sweet Jesus. I say yes. Will you say yes too and usher in a revival beginning with me beginning with you…

Oh Happy Day

oh happy day the song goes

the day Jesus came and took

my sins away,

sweet rejoicing in the by and by,

oh happy, happy day,

no more sadness no more tears,

He has them held within the flask,

beauty for ashes,

joy for mourning,

at the rising of the sun,

he sees you there waiting for Him,

He walks pass and you see His shadow,

falling upon you,

the shadow of the almighty,

resting on you… right there…

where you are

the moment… your God moment…

His grace….

right there... where you are

surrender to Him,

Oh sweet happy day,

all your longings..

Now gone,

HE.... the Author of YOU,

the creator of YOU,

in your midst,

behold how great…

how great is our God…

Oh sweet happy, happy day.

Jude 1:24-25 To him who is able to keep you from falling and to present you before His glorious presence without fault and with great JOY- to the only God our Savior be glory, majesty, power and authority, through Jesus Christ our Lord, before all ages, now and forevermore! Amen.

Revival

I feel a revival coming,

sweeping through the land,

here… it begins with me…

with you…,

we cry Lord come,

fall upon us,

we've awaken from our

stupor,

we are here steadfast,

waiting for you,

calling for you,

the fire is burning,

and we are yearning for your

touch,

Holy Spirit… let your fire

fall,

anew in our midst,

within the deepest

corridor

of our being,

fresh anointing,

of a double portion,

overflow within us,

till there is no flesh,

and only Spirit's

left,

spreading within us

a flame,

a passion for holiness,

that we live and move

ever in your presence,

and all that pass,

will catch the flame,

burning with

revival,

let it spread,

and let it begin

with me…

An Opus

music... so very beautiful,

timing... rhythm...lyrics and such...

you want the moment,

He longs to give it to you,

working behind the scenes of

your life,

He is the great orchestrator,

of a master piece in which,

you are the instrument,

the music, the chords,

the art,

in which He fashions for the world,

an opus so amazingly graced,

He wants to play a love song,

for all to hear,

because you are His handiwork,

anointed and blessed,

and all will see you...

and listen to the song,

He made from your life,

working behind the scenes…

,orchestrating…

Composing…

your life…

a beautiful

beautiful

song…

Come on In and Sit Awhile

come on in and sit awhile,

here…right at my feet,

come on in to the throne

of grace,

no need to bang at the gate,

it is open just for you,

come be my guest,

I long for you to visit,

here… near where I am

petition me and we can

talk

I'll tell you all you need

to know,

I love you dear child,

i have a feast awaiting here,

just for you,

that will satisfy your

soul,

come on in and sit awhile,

I'll tell you all about,

your home I'm building

just for you

here in the by and by,

tell me what you need,

I long to give you gifts,

gives me great joy,

to listen for a while.

I am your Abba Father,

come to me and rest,

beneath my feet,

and sit awhile,

I'll give you all

you need

and more,

only come and sit,

we need to talk...

An Idol

there's an idol set before you,

but you cannot understand,

right there in your midst,

you don't know what it is,

It's that desire pulling at

your heart,

whispering put me first,

the dream...

the passion for

something other than.....

HIM...

alone...you take out your

idol,

and you bow and worship it,

fashioned neither of silver,

nor of gold,

but it's there....right before you,

exalted higher than His Name.

You deny that it is so,

but each morning you awake...

it's not the Lord...

you put first… but this thing,

this thought,

on a platform....elevated above

the Most High.

give it up and put Him first,

and no longer will the idol,

control your very life,

and God will shine ever brighter,

and the desire once an idol…

will be given as a gift...

from God

The Inner War

there's a war going on,

deep within my soul today,

don't know what to do,

confused for the moment,

my flesh tells me keep it up,

the Spirit says take it down,

my spirit longs to please God,

my flesh tells me otherwise,

just a little attention,

speaks my inner man,

yet... the still small voice,

tells me of another plan,

the more excellent way,

my flesh cries out,

ME,

My spirit cries out

GOD,

it's hard to know what's

really right,

when sins not soo big,

creep in,

if it's sin at all,

that's where I'm torn,

and I know the biggest part

of me,

longs to please the Master,

I gave Him my all today,

yet this struggle has me broken,

to know the more excellent way,

I long to be loved and

consider…

that I could have another,

years of hurt and pain,

has dissolved into peace,

and really nothing other,

and yet I find that I

struggle with two paths

along my journey,

moments away from

total freedom,

yet… I think I'd like a lover,

nothing sinful nor impure,

just a sense of completeness,

and eventually one,

bonded to each other,

as one flesh,

but now I am just so torn…

I Choose Life

i choose life,

obedience,

the lifting of my hands

as the morning sacrifice,

I call Him Lord, Lord,

and He does so here me,

I His daughter bow

before Him and I choose

Life,

so often death has

come along,

to trip me up,

but now I choose

Him,

and His Word shall

abide in me forever,

old man now dead,

surrendered to the one,

new man Jesus Christ,

new life abundant rain,

waters overflow,

in a once parch desert,

I choose life,

I choose Him,

I will give my all,

my gift,

myself,

wholly surrendered,

at His altar

If I Put Down the Idol

God's telling me put it down,

if I do will he return it

as a gift,

I want to put down the idol,

for He is more precious than

diamonds,

want to be like Solomon,

in wisdom,

and know and walk,

in the light of His

countenance,

I think I will put down,

the idol..

and not look back,

to be turned into stone,

I will wait upon

Him

who gives us all things,

in His timing,

I will delight in Him,

and my heart's desire,

granted before me,

I will sing praise,

and wait upon the Lord

as I now put down the idol...

Then God

Then God,

Only God,

Forever God,

Today God,

Tomorrow God,

Eternally God,

Here God,

Now God,

Choose God,

Believe God,

Trust God,

Know God,

True God,

MY life,

In God,

No other,

But God,

Alone.

There is GOD...

I Am Alone In the Storm

I am alone,

lonely,

frightened by

the storm,

the waves,

are high,

and I can't

seem to swim,

the coast so

far,

and I fearful,

of today,

tomorrow,

draws nigh,

the lies

ever stronger,

I am alone,

and lonely,

worried about

tomorrow,

gasping,

trying

to stay afloat,

no-one hears,

sees… nor cares,

enough to send,

the life boat,

some try to come,

and see that

I barely reach,

enough to grab

a hold of them,

they leave and

I am here beneath,

the waves drowning,

drowning beneath

the water,

unconscious

I go,

if only I could

breathe,

then I could live

I think I'm drowning…

The Floggings - The Cross

weighed down by your sins,

Jesus died for you

nailed between two thieves,

they flogged Him,

persecuted Him,

spit upon His face,

nailed upon the cross,

by the religious ones,

who are they,

that persecute you

beat you down,

with a load of cares,

accusers of your sin,

point and sneer

you try to run,

no place to hide,

with the load of

cares,

angered by yourself,

the condition of

the past,

you flog yourself,

until you bleed,

nailing yourself,

to your own rugged

cross,

till you can't ....

bare the voice

of the one,

who accuses you,

and writes your name

for all to see,

casting stones,

you feel exposed,

so you flog yourself,

till you're punished enough

for your misdeed,

you look to others,

to look and see,

that you are stripped,

and naked,

filled with blood,

and you ask with your heart... do you think

I'm okay?

Longing to be approved,

you flog yourself,

nailed to your

self made cross,

by the others...

of religiosity,

yet... the floggings..

need not be,

though your accusers are

many,

As David...

stone in hand,

swung that sling,

and it did land,

and knocked that giant down,

the death...

that Jesus did die,

He died for me,

He died for all,

that we need not

flog ourselves,

nor suffer upon

our self-made cross,

He took the floggings

the cross,

did bare the sins

for me and you,

that is when our

giant fell,

when Jesus rose

again,

Victory…

Standing

standing, standing,

forever strong,

bold and courageous.

In Him,

I trust,

as He enfolds

my being,

I can stand,

on His forever

Word,

of life,

In me

He lives,

and dwells,

makes His abode,

encamps within

my temple,

standing, standing,

forever strong,

with His word,

in hand,

He takes my

every care,

within His hold,

and here

I can stand,

knowing He has my

very being,

within His eternal

grasp,

never to be shaken,

standing forever strong

Acknowledge

acknowledge before God,

your sin

and choose

the course before you,

remind yourself,

from whence

you came,

and how He

drew you out,

by His Word,

forget not,

His kindness,

in the day,

nor His goodness.

in the night,

acknowledge before

God and man,

the deeds that brought

you down,

that they might see,

His hand of grace,

that delivers

a sinner that

goes astray,

ordering his

steps

another way,

till He safely leads

him home…

Deception

comes in the night

he's the angel of light.

so charming…

yet deceptive

is he,

he comes to draw you,

captivate you,

with his poetic

way,

he's an angel

alright,

angel of the night,

he entraps you,

then engulfs your

mind.

you think he's okay,

till he pulls you

astray,

from your once firm

foundation,

then he rips at your heart

and tears you apart,

then says you are not

right in your faith,

till your knees both

grow weak

as you believe

every lie,

said against you,

once so endeared,

now the man

that you fear,

tells you

he knows you so

well

till you have lost

yourself,

and know not what you are,

and have fallen from

your faith,

so deceived,

by the lie,

that he speaks

with his mouth

till you turn

from his voice,

and look and

live to the

one who

died so the

voice of deception,

can die that eternal

damnation...

Could I Have Your Attention Please Dear God,

He says YES, plug away I am always here. Nothing you could do or say will take me away from you.

I never sleep and never slumber. I am here at the midnight hour. I am here at the crack of dawn.

You never have to wait on line.

I will never put you on hold.

I will never have voice mail and I will always open the knock on my door.

I will be here when everyone else has left town.

I will be here when you need a shoulder to cry on. You have my attention at all times. I love you like a father loves his

cute little girl in pigtails.

We are the apple of His eye and we could never ask for too much attention. He is here, there and everywhere that you

are and that you go.

So, plug away you have HIS ATTENTION. Speak or forever hold your peace

Never In Your Wildest Dreams

never in your wildest dreams

would you...

have ever fathomed,

something so wonderful,

an arrangement just for you,

flowers from heaven,

the bouquet,

sent with love for you

by God,

filled with peace, joy,

hope and abundance of rain,

for spiritual blossoms,

cherished moments,

created and sprinkled

with angels breath,

endued with mists of

loveliness,

never in your wildest dreams,

fancied in fantasy,

could you create,

such a lovely arrangement,

handpicked by your Lover with

Love for YOU...

Run With The Vision

run with the vision,

ever before you,

let it drive,

consume your being,

speak it,

breathe it,

live it,

speak the words from

within...

without...

let your voice...

encapsulate,

the fashion ...

of your dreams,

the skeleton,

comes alive,

bones endued

with flesh,

God says now...

come alive...

to the hope...

reality of...

the vision.

now alive...

in you...

now come...

to pass...

in you...

vision

Voices

voices, voices one said he

heard voices,

from behind, saying this

is the way,

walk thou in it,

roads, roads, the voice

said follow the road,

guiding, leading, revealing

the way,

the straight path, the narrow

road, stretching for

miles, miles on end,

voices, voices leading him on,

many were troubled by the voices

he heard,

wondered, how strange a man,

can that be,

voices, voices leading him on,

terrors by day, fears and worries

by night, still voices, voices,

cheering him on,

so close, so close, to home

my dear child,

voices, voices say "fight the good fight."

Battle the lies, walk strong and

be firm,

hold on to the weapon,

and fight and fight,

till the end.

voices, voices speak from behind…

the battle the battle, the battle

is won!!

voices, voices the army of God,

dressed for the fight,

as they sing through the night,

the battle the battle the battle

is won, the voices the voices

ever so clear, leaded and guided,

to the fate that is here.

Heaven awaits your entrance

my dear…

People Say

People have a lot to say,

about your today and tomorrow,

they haven't walked within your shoes,

nor have they trudged along your path,

they just have a lot to say about your

today and tomorrow,

The righteous… the proud… come along

by your side,

and whisper such and such

and this and that,

thus sayeth the Lord,

till your standing there

scratching your head,

wondering… is that what Jesus would

have said,

opinions and such could make you..

stand on your head,

from the confusion and craziness

you feel

when six well-mannered Christians…

intentions so good…

have given you six different paths you

should take,

and you stand there and just shake your

head,

as only you could do,

people say and they say and they say,

give me a break…

perhaps…

I should listen and let..

God show me the way,

and I don't want to hear

what the good people say,

for the one on the right

did beat his chest

and the Lord knew …

his heart right away.

while the other so proudly…

did intercede

and said what a good boy am I,

but the other went away,

fully forgiven as

he humbled himself that day,

The Day We Said Good-Bye

the day we said good bye,

was the day I lived again,

unequally yoked brought a

weight of sin,

within my heart that wore me

down,

and heavy was my soul,

I could not shake at times,

the heaviness within,

you pressed and many times

had your way,

selfish desires that went

against my souls ambition,

to please the master of

my being,

grief… anguish..

my soul

yielding at times

to the temptation,

but... then I woke up

and said... "No more"

shall I enter into sin,

and bow my knee to that

which brings death... to a walk

that beckons me to come

and enter in...

I put down the imagination

that yielded to another way,

other than the revelation

of who God is

and His perfect plan for

me to walk upright,

and say good bye

to such things

which lead me down

the other way,

not so clear..

distant

from the Love I long

to have

enveloped in Him

the day we said good bye

I began again

to rise up within

the true me,

and live again

for Him…

What a Mighty God We Serve

what a mighty God we serve,

with ashes right before you,

He sweeps them all away,

replaced the oil,

to light the candle,

that grew dim,

what a mighty God we serve,

with blessing on every bend,

once mourning cast its ugly

frown,

now blessings shouting all

around.

cleaned the home once,

filled with dust,

old sins,

now gone,

what a mighty God we serve,

new paintings all about,

fine white linens standing out,

the scene so changed from

a time before,

what a mighty God we serve

windows clear to see the dove

fly by,

perched upon the nearby sill

resting there to let me know

what a mighty God we serve,

the Holy Spirit dwelling here,

His perfect love..

ever whispering... in my ear,

only know.... what a mighty God

we serve.....parting Seas...

knocking down walls...

What a mighty God we serve...

Life is But a Dream

if the world were but a dream

what would it configure,

morning glories, and daffodils,

hills and hills of endless glory,

rolling ever yonder,

there beside a flowing brook,

a never ending gentle stream,

leads into the valley,

looking up you see the sun

shine.. through the breaks

between the trees,

eagles fly above the clouds,

spreading wings that glide

through the air,

below the waters move...

as tiny fish collect as one,

lily pads and wonders such,

steal your breath away,

still more beauty up ahead,

approaching colors move your

world,

pastels bring a gentle calm,

showered by the morning mist,

perennials etched in cluttered

patterns,

elegantly arise above the fashion,

splendor dances all around,

fills the world with moments,

to think and hope and live

for life is really

but a dream..

If You Don't Know

if you don't know what you're doing,

i surely don't,

just kinda shrugging my shoulders,

don't know... just don't know,

where are you going to running so fast?

Don't know... just don't know,

what are you doing? Going here and there?

Don't know... just don't know.

just kinda walking and shrugging right along,

don't know... just don't know,

can't really help you

don't know where you're going... never mind

what you're doing.

looking for answers to your questions

can't seem to solve them,

moving right along,

if you don't know what you are doing

I suggest you wait awhile,

sit down a bit,

and hold on to your feelings,

until you know what's the better way,

because if you don't know what you're doing,

I surely don't,

hardly have a handle on my own

path I travel,

look up my silly friend,

and I will look up too,

perhaps God will lead us on,

and we will find our way,

Dead in the Dead Sea

Praising God,...Oh Glory!!

Got baptized in the Jordan,

sins been washed away,

going to the dead sea,

as dead as dead can be,

I went under... got raised...

a new creation,

death went yonder.. going in

the Jordan,

all my sins have been washed away,

dead and gone in the dead sea,

to be remembered never more,

the old man died,

never to be resurrected,

it's dead and gone,

drowned out all my sorrows,

flowing into the dead sea,

as dead as dead can be,

before I felt so heavy,

but now I am feeling lighter,

now that the old man,

has been taken down,

I feel a whole lot brighter,

because that man is dead and gone,

over there in the dead sea,

where my sins are thrown,

to never be remembered,

I came alive in the Jordan,

and the old me can stay dead

in THE DEAD SEA!!!

Empty Things With Empty Moments

when the world is so full of empty moments,

and life seems to have passed you by,

you wonder what tomorrow brings,

underneath the starry skies,

a wish in your heart of what might be,

or could be or whatever your mind

wonders to,

is okay I guess for it is just

imaginary moments filled with empty

vanity,

you look out into space… hoping

to stumble across the answers,

to what just kind of passed you by,

it was empty moments.. no memories

to think of,

you would never fantasize about going

back,

to the dark world in which you left

but still life is so filled with empty

moments,

shallow passing of time,

things with no purpose,

that trickle the days away,

when this world smiles at your moments,

it leaves you so very empty inside,

and what you think will make a change,

never really fills the void,

with what you hoped it would,

just traveling and marching

through time,

no meaning has spoken to your heart,

and purpose has not yet knocked at your door,

to let it in and make its abode,

within the shadows of your life,

and rainbows never appear,

when you so want to see one,

and tomorrow is filled with

empty things.

We The Beloved

We the beloved,

called by His name,

measured by no ruler,

day to day the same,

He calls us His beloved,

each morning we arise,

He whispers I love you,

as the breeze whistles

through the window pain,

and the sun smiles brightly

in the heavens...

as we look out..

from our resting place,

we know that we are His,

as we call to Him...

Abba...Abba...

sweet Abba

Father,

He bends down to listen,

ever so near to us children,

He scoops us up,

into His presence we stay,

for a while... and bathe

in His love... for we

are called by His name,

we are His beloved...

children... we are...

The Enemy

the enemy of your soul,

is after you,

trying to enslave you to his way...

of thinking... and decreasing,

the thoughts that God has

planted in your heart,

robbing the purpose,

the joy that is just

for you,

taking captive your heart...

to this world,

you're trapped within,

the concepts of this place,

and time,

empty and alone

afraid of tomorrow,

the shadows of yesterday,

leaves a veil.. Not able

to be lifted... and you

are lonely... listening

to the voice...that tells

you the world... is so empty

and purposeless,

and you stay there in

that place alone, and

wondering the purpose

for the way you feel

and the enemy is loving it…

just the way you are,

You're all alone... Listening

to his every lie.

never realizing the cross

before you...

the one who hung there

so very long ago

is calling out to you...

to listen to Him

and join with his heart

and close your ears

to the enemy...

who longs to

rob your life of

everything that God

has given to you,

answer the call to truth

and in due season thou shalt

reap if thou faint not..

Come into the higher

place and let not your

enemy win

and listen not…

but be true to Him

and He will be faithful

to raise you up to

higher ground

Rainbows Chasing Rainbows

rainbows just chasing rainbows

in the sky as I glide through

this life of stormy weather

grey clouds give way to sunshine

as I walk through streets

wet from the rain

drops fall upon me

and I feel cold

but I see the sun peeking through

the cloudiness

gives way to sunshine

as the rays warms me

I see a rainbow

reminds me of the promise

He once made

rainbows just chasing rainbows

in the sky as I glide through

this life of stormy weather

I know He is near

as the clouds clear

and color comes to my world

the Rainbow appears and it's

so beautiful

joy finds a way

enlightening the dark precepts of the mind

chasing rainbows… just chasing rainbows

knowing that one belongs to you

all is well

Twists Twists Twists and Turns

twists, twists, twists and turns,

leaves you spinning evermore,

you wake up...

nothings quite the same,

changes, changes at your door,

leaves such stirring in your soul,

up, down, nothing sound,

like tornadoes spinning

round and round,

fears within,

keep you running all about,

questions, doubts, anxiety,

have you falling to your knees,

the cross, the cross, Jesus Christ..

You must hold on,

nothing more,

the answer's there...

in the blood,

waiting, waiting, He's waiting

for you...

touch the robe,

touch His hand,

healing's there within the plan,

though pressed down..

confusion all around,

He speaks "Peace Be Still"

and the Storm subsides,

rest, rest all about,

Peace and Love...

now reigns within,

there inside...

lives the three

in one,

Never To Be Forsaken

Though you might have been forsaken. Always rejoice. For it is the storms that prove our faith. That is our strength and our character comes from such storms of life. If we never had a storm nor a trial how would we come to know how great a salvation we truly have. We come to know faith and live the faith walk through the testings that come to pull us from such a glorious walk in Christ Jesus. Put on joy and smile every time the enemy comes around. You are getting even one more step closer to great faith. The faith of our fathers, such faith would change this generation. Think of the trials of Moses and Abraham, just at the brink of destruction faith stepped in and showed its power. It is the darkest before the dawning of a great day. So, I say rejoice always and again I say rejoice.

Moved

moved by a spirit

outside of me,

touched a hand,

I could not see,

felt a presence,

I longed to hold,

encapsulated by

the awe of it,

groans within

me,

cannot explain,

the depths so deep,

only he could touch,

felt a feeling,

not to share,

entered a place,

no-one can reach,

inspired by the voice...

moved my soul,

to know...

he is there...

just...

moved

He's Still There

he's still there

though you

have stepped away,

to find your place,

kind a like a friend you

haven't spoken to,

for such a while,

you call him…

back and he"s still,

your friend… just distant

for a while,

you catch up,

and know he'll

always be there,

so close once,

you knew His very

heart,

but you stepped away,

Jesus waits…Oh yes…

He waits…dearer and

closer than any friend,

could ever be,

He's there in your heart,

and you know and feel,

You are so aware,

He's there,

to be your dearest friend,

again...

He waits. He's still there...

Call Him,

He longs to talk,

and be close again,

with you,

a friend far closer than

even a brother,

He's everything...

your everything

Where Are You Going Along This Journey

where are you going along this journey?

which path do you follow?

so many choices.

makes you wonder,

about the challenges,

the crossroads

forks and such,

bends along the way

makes your mind go

blank…

for meaning

purpose and direction

so vague,

skies cloudy,

rain falls,

and the calling

flooded by skepticism,

gets your vision,

rushing down a winding

river,

as you follow the rapids along

the banks,

it's hard to keep the pace,

as you chase along,

hoping it would

flow into a stream,

and you could catch,

the hope of rescuing

what you were meant

to become,

it vanished so quickly,

going along this journey,

so confused about the choices,

decisions as to roads and

paths... lost sight

of the calling,

running... running to

catch up,

perhaps the stream,

a brook approaches,

and you could capture

the moments again,

and regain your strength,

to get on the narrow road,

and find your way,

to where you were meant

to be..

On this journey Home,

In The Spirit Of Writing

In the spirit of writing tonight,

alone in my quiet world…

all alone,

just thinking of such and such,

and pondering such deep thoughts,

in this spirit of writing,

thinking of moments and the meaning

of life,

the purpose and reality of existence,

philosophically defining..

reasoning's outside

of myself,

to whys and why nots,

and the deeper things,

that to some might not matter,

I wonder about tomorrow,

as today winds down to

a yesterday,

thinking if today

defined

a clear purpose,

and if tomorrow will

bring a change,

sitting on the sidelines,

waiting for answers,

as I step into directions

unclear as of yet,

long to answer a call,

I had some time ago,

not sure what it is,

as I philosophically,

think the deeper thoughts,

I'm waiting for the

moment to fall..

into place,

in the spirit of writing,

looking up and just

pondering,

what exactly the purpose was,

and if perhaps I missed,

the call I was...

suppose to answer,

did it ring and

I had not heard,

was the voice so

quiet,

that I got caught up

in other things,

the shallow side,

of living,

well… I wait. I wait…

for Him,

to stir anew,

the fire,

and burn it ever

brighter,

then when it

had first begun,

years ago,

the vision

the calling

the anointing,

burn in me

afresh,

that the

purpose will

arise,

and I will be

what I was

designed,

fashioned

meant to be

before the

foundations

of the earth,

just waiting.

and hoping,

today,

it might

begin,

and I could

live and know

that I am

living,

for Him,

and not myself

and myself..

Alone...

Dear God....

Moments

The moments take me away,

and I am caught up

I feel that they are all

my own,

I don't want

them to leave me now,

it felt safe for the time,

nestled in a cozy spot,

just listening to the fantasy

of it all,

swept me away and the moments,

passed ever so quickly,

and now I wonder,

why it had to go

at such a time

as this,

when I am now kind

of ready to

be swept away,

I liked the way it was,

in the moments alone

wishing and thinking,

about the beauty of

it all,

in those moments l

alone

in my quiet place,

stretched out and

wishing,

it would never

go away,

such moments don't

come so very often,

and I cherish moments

such as these,

and I pray,

let them come again

the moments..

The Enemy

when the enemy comes in like a flood,

He will lift up a standard against it,

when the strong wind blows,

Stand...

when the storms rage against you,

Stand,

when the fires threaten to consume you,

Stand,

when the foundations beneath you trembles,

Stand,

when the worlds chaos beats against your mind...

again I say

Stand,

Stand firm and stand strong,

for the times might beat against you

and you feel there is no

hope,

Stand my brother stand,

for a mighty fortress have we...

stand, stand, stand,

and don't sit for anything.

raise your banner high,

and lift your hands as

Moses at the parting of

the Red Sea,

stand for your deliverance

draweth nigh...

Oh it is in the greatest storms of life that He shines ever brighter... Only know that He is there and here and everywhere. Only stand firm and believe and your Red Sea shall part and what a walk, a sweet walk to the other side...

When We're Walking In The Night

when we're walking in the night,

no light around,

and darkness seems to be all there is,

hold on,

we can get through,

just a prayer away,

tis true,

when the candle burns,

and only wax remains,

the light,

has burned out,

we're walking in the night,

we feel the slip along the way,

getting to the other side,

of our vision,

and hope,

is dark for the moment,

hold on,

tis true,

just...but a prayer away,

sweet light,

dark night,

is gone...

when we're walking in the night,

hold on,

hope...faith is what

we have only to see

us through

Valleys Rivers and Streams

valleys rivers and streams,

wildflowers trail the patchy

scene,

animals visible between the

breaks within,

the trees,

shades of evergreens,

and sunlight that peaks

it's light,

the glimpse

of rays,

warms your countenance

natures lulling,

imagery,

paints your world

with simplistic,

longings for that...

world...

of what life

was meant to be,

in its fullness

when Love created,

that first river,

valley and stream,

when mankind

tilled the soil,

and fruit bore

after its kind,

and multiplied

upon the earth,

such love and

care,

enveloped...

in passion...

The Sound of Silence

the sound of silence,

deep...dark...silence,

filled the room,

no sound.

yet quite

the sound of the empty

heart that filled it,

taken back from what once

seemed like music to an

ear that was apparently

soundly deaf,

for the music was a vibration

that quite sincerely was

dead and no dance followed it,

none at all....

it was the sound of silence...

the deepest entrance of her soul,

had no notes to play,

no song to sing...just merely

a dead beat of utter disaster... again...

silence...

alone. but...

trapped in silence...

dead...numb

within herself she screamed...no one could hear

because there was no voice...

just silence...

no-one listens....

for she's silent..

paralyzed by what could be

and what should be...

the sound of silence...

controls her world..

no-one understands the state...

of her silence...

trapped in the sound of silence

And Together They Walked

and together they walked to the assembly,

yet alone she was by his side.

arm in arm...he smiled at her...

along the dark and dreary trail,

that lead the way to the place...

called worship...he held his hands

so very high,

she meekly humbled a prayer of plea...

to see beyond the here and now...

her head dropped. In shame...

she remembered...when she thought

she knew...NOW darkness only...

the crimson lie ever

clearer...clearer than before...

used...she is... and ashy stains beneath

her eyes...tell another story...

of the two who walked the path...

to gather amongst the brothers...

twice the pain...twice the blow...

thou foul angel of light.

who left the crimson stain...

walking by her side...

he worships ever louder...

disguised in such Godly attire...

dripping blood from his lips...

no-one sees the devour...

that ripped apart her.soul...

and together...yet...they walked...

in the midst of the congregation...

one dark and evil...there with hands

stretched out..

blended...the evil and dark amongst...

the children of God...

yet...they knew...

no rescue she

thought...as she cried....

BUT...BUT God...

HE COMES....

and then...

Love At All Cost

love at all cost,

let the past stay where

it may,

there's the rising of the

new day,

fear can be gone and hope

will...and can arise,

if you let it... and choose...

you must grab it,

and hold it tightly,

cling to the little trust

that dwells within your...

very being...

trust...hope. Love

faith will see you through,

and you can face tomorrow...

knowing... that Love... will meet you

The Wind

Where the wind blows,

one cannot tell,

where it might carry

you,

away... perhaps...

tornado winds,

hurricane winds,

ocean breeze,

gentle soothing wind,

sounds of the voice...

of God...

you feel the wind,

gentle at times..

soothing your

spirit,

other times

thrashing,

like a torrent,

shaken... the very

place you stand,

once thought to be

solid ground,

upsweeps you

and you are caught in

the whirlwind,

spinning….ever wondering

the way out...

the wind thrashes

you around and you

cannot see through

the fog,

dark clouds...

windy, windier,

blasting wind,

and trashing wind.

no-one can

see you in the

wind. hopefully,

you do not crash...

the wind beats you

against the circumstances...

the never ending circumstance.

that beat you

and finally hopefully

the sun might one day come out

and no more wind

it ceases for the time

and then there is that

gentle ocean breeze.

Me and You Against the World

Dear God,

It's me and you against the world,

just me and you…lost mostly everything,

Yet… I know I still have you

and the me is not alone,

because there will

always be You,

and me against the world,

The chastisement of the Lord is not pleasant and when you enter the valley it is quite deep. When one thinks of a valley there is no easy access out and the only real way out is to climb and the climb can be treacherous. But as the bible says there is the valley of Achor which has the door of hope. Trying to climb on either side of the valley is difficult and scary but once one starts climbing eventually one gets to the top of that ole mountain. So, tell me.... keep climbing and I will tell you.... keep climbing Jimmy Dean.

The Valley

so, I found myself in the Valley,

tried to take a road on my own,

cliffs were high and the edge had

no barrier,

and I felt as though I would fall,

I cried.. oh Lord I'm trippin!!

on the idea that I'm totally gone

so, I took on another road just

around the bend,

and discovered that was wrong too,

I asked different people

along the way,

Is this the road I should be taking?

and they lead me further astray,

the road got more frightening,

until I discovered it was just

me alone,

where I was...was no network,

no strangers nor friends to be found,

and I cried out dear Lord,

I'm now down in the Valley,

Alone...

nobody to call. the strangers wouldn't even

know nor lead me to the

way HOME.

for my home is long gone,

because I am here stuck in

the Valley.

And there's no-one to call...

I cry out Jesus!

here in my Valley

alone... God help. I don't know

which way to go anymore...

Come My Child

He says… come to the fountain and drink,

those who are thirsty and sink,

beneath the miry clay,

the mud and the stains,

that bathe you each day,

leaves one unable to reach…

for the cool refreshing…

waters of life,

left now… all dirty and dry,

by the world …lacking

rivers of water so clear,

The Lord says… Come my child,

Come… to the waters…

Drink…Drink…

and never be thirsty again….

I long to fill you with life

and give you all that you need

to never be dry again.

Crosswords and Bridges

crossroads and bridges.

and forks we cannot bare,

He leads me on the narrow path

squeezed...fearfully… you see... the answer

is there,

pressing me at every angle,

calling and beckoning me onward,

homeward bound,

the bridges are weak,

as I look down below,

I could feel the thoughts of drowning,

neither foot has touched

the waters though..

forks… preventing me from

following the road,

the voice calls me

to walk… He has already tread

the way...

crossroads come pointing

left and then right,

all through the night,

the dim light never shines

down quite bright enough.

fear in the choosing

for choices have

outcomes

crossroads and bridges

that beckon

decision...

Grace to choose the

right path...

Pray that the path will shine brighter and I will follow it correctly.

God Help

God help when the questions wail against my thoughts,

and I wrestle against my flesh

which pounds against my being,

my mind screams for answers to crossroads,

that twist the condition of my mind,

I beat the wind and the Holy Spirit

is speaking...yet.. I cannot hear

my ears are clogged with

wants and wishes

like a wax

that prevents

truth to get in...

something I think

tells me to go this way,

yet...I say... that cannot be

the road...

He wants for me....

so...again I beat against

the flesh and it does not want

to listen...

ohhh... the flogging like the priests.

the pain is not letting me

let go...

I beat myself some more to

want to hear the answer...

is it my voice that keeps me

in pain...

or God that is trying

to release me from whatever...

is my will..

to bring me into His...

perfect union,

either road is hard

it now seems...

I ponder...

which might be the road less

traveled...an which is the choice

to bring me Home..?

Help...Dear God

Forest

In the forest alone,

walking along the trails,

I am fascinated by the streams,

the waterfalls tranquilize me

as I stroll along the paths,

filled with mystic wonder,

laughter fills my heart,

as I see something scurry by,

nature... such an intricate

part of God's design,

takes me away to serenity,

smiles boil over... as my heart,

is captured by the breaks between

the trees, as the sun peeps through

the spaces and gaps, and the leaves,

arrayed in splendor of color,

reminds me of the promise,

God had made while,

coloring the sky with

eccentric rainbow design,

and the stars we see,

camping underneath the

darkened sky. Here in the forest,

alone with my maker...

Venom

In the corners of my mind,

the sad moments,

I can't define,

speechless...absorbed in

thoughts... stuck

within the cobwebs,

entangled in fears,

of being swallowed,

by the black widow...

my anxious being.

struggling to know the

way of escape...

from the being that

rolls and rolls the web

ever tighter around my

person...squeezing ever

tighter and I choke

because the solution..

the venom has me

losing control...

Of Life.

Doing the Esther Fast

Doing the Esther Fast,

no food no drink,

just me and God,alone alas,

lies and such,

dissipate,

doing the Esther Fast,

weapons carnal,

never mind,

our warfare.

is spiritual,

not flesh, not blood,

breaking and destroying,

the enemies plans,

doing the Esther Fast,

satan be gone,

demons destroyed,

by the Word of my testimony,

just lovin..doing the Esther Fast,

no need of food of worldly pleasure,

getting stronger each time

I do the Esther Fast,

My God knows how

hungry I am,

For Him and Him alone

Doing the Esther Fast

Lord... Lord

We call Him Lord..Lord but then we go our way..

all we like sheep keep goin astray...

just risen in the morning.. layin in the night..

but our lives just aint right.

our hearts cry.. THE HEART OF THE FATHER..

The Great Lover...

of our soul...

have mercy on us...and be the guidance that we need…

we shall not seek another...sister nor a brother.

we have Abba Father...let His will be done.

let us not run amiss.

searchin for answers...when He has all the answers

that our hearts long for.

He is the Way, the Truth and the Life…

He is our only Hope…

The Door.

our entrance..

into His Kingdom..

distractions and all life's reactions to moments passing..

quickly...we are moving and time beats quickly..

and our purpose is ever before us... and we must be ever

reaching…

avoiding...ignoring..those venomous demons...

pulling us in directions...away and astray...from our calling..

divine appointments...leading…guiding...drawing us in...

to purpose...

light to light...keep your eyes on the prize...clog your ears to lies…

don't despise...your gift...cling to the Master...time is going faster...faster...time is running out…

have faith.

don't doubt...line upon line...precept upon precept...

keep pluggin away...look not to the left...nor to the right..

fight..fight…fight the fight of faith

run with the dream.. the vision...stirring you on...keep reaching...you are almost there...don't let go of His cloak..His anointing will provide your lack...fear will hold you back

IGNORE THE DISTRACTIONS to fear...doubt...lack and anything that prevents that Divine Calling...you will soon be home.

Abba's waiting…make Him proud...the work will be completed...that which He called you to do...

So Amazing

it's just amazing..

when I think about His love...

towards me..

when I am alone with Him..

in that quiet place.

Him and I face to face.

I don't need to be afraid.

there's no-one watching me..

and I am free to worship..

at His feet..

no-one can judge whether..

I am worthy...or not..

but it's my lot....

in this life..

to be the bride of Christ.

and He dresses me in white..

and I am new..

and pure as freshly

fallen snow.

although at times I make

mistakes..

my hearts desire..

is His embrace.

and when He holds this

fragile heart...

my spirit man can sweetly smile..

because all along the journey..

this spirit, soul and body,

is truly panting after Him...

The Secret Place

sometimes its a secret.

a moment all alone.

.just me and God.

He wants me to himself..

and no one needs to know.

just Him and I alone.

no one to impress

He gets all the glory..

its really His story.

not mine.

He is the potter..

and I am the clay

He's creator of this masterpiece

the awesome playwright..

all rights

belong to the writer of this script.

He wants all the Glory.

and none belongs to me.

Let me meet my Love in Secret.

its these closet moments.

that He truly appreciates.

drawing me closer.

It's not about my glory.

though I have a testimony

and that I need to share.

but intimate moments

with my Father..

It's just Him and Him alone

Shaken the Pillars

standing on the backline

sitting on the sideline

trying to define

my space in time

looking for the clear line

as time rushes by

wishing I could fly

never wanted to die

but I find myself

dying every day

tryin...tryin...

to hold on

to the Way

the Truth...the Life...

from Christ...

I hold so dear...

knowin He is near...

on my path

so unclear...

guiding me...

as I blindly follow...

like Sampson...

defeated for awhile..

enduring the trial…

the mocking…the beating…

feeling defeated…

a final cry…

for the anointing…

to overtake the vessel…

as I wrestle with demons…

who rob my blessing…

one last blow…

as I surrender…

completely…

for 9 billion souls…

I claim for Jesus…

with an overcoming victory…

shaking the pillars..

pleading at His altar…

principalities defeated…

I can see…

Jesus…Jesus… has made

the decree…

Winner….

A Love Letter To My Lord

Let me write a love letter to my Lord…

Tell Him how much I adore

Him…

Oh how He moves my soul…

To be held in His presence…

My lips cannot help but praise

Him…

Glory in who He is…

The Great I Am…

Before I ever existed…

He knew…

Before I ever had a will…

That I would love Him…

I say now and throughout

Eternity…

Basking in His Love…

Is all I ever really wanted…

All I ever needed…

He…Jesus…The Great I Am…

Shekinah…Shekinah Glory

Fall on me..

For I love you…and your presence

Is all this heart ever needed…

To be complete…

Complete in You…

Oh Lord…How I love you…

So I write this love letter

Just for you…

Because I love everything that you are…

Oh Great I Am…

Shepard and lover of my soul…

The whole of me I give to you…

Only let me bask in your presence…

In your Shekinah Glory…

Oh Epikazoa overshadow me…

Til I be no more….

But only filled with your presence..

Let your Glory fill me….

I love you…the Great Lover of my soul…

I write..I write this love letter just for you…

I love you dear Lord and thank you for the journey that led me straight to you.

All along the journey the Father is calling us to Himself. We become His children when we receive His Son Jesus as Lord and Savior. He is far better than any earthly father can ever be. He loves us unconditionally. He is our constant guide and when we choose the wrong path He lovingly corrects us by showing us the way. He is constantly speaking to us and longs to have an intimate relationship with each of His children. Though the way at times can be unsettling He is teaching us to trust in Him. When life seems its toughest He's asking us to draw closer to Him. He wants to wrap us in His arms and comfort us with His presence for He is Abba the great lover of our soul.

Romans 8: 15-19 KJV

[15] For ye have not received the spirit of bondage again to fear; but ye have received the Spirit of adoption, whereby we cry, Abba, Father. [16] The Spirit itself beareth witness with our spirit, that we are the children of God: [17] And if children, then heirs; heirs of God, and joint-heirs with Christ; if so be that we suffer with him, that we may be also glorified together. [18] For I reckon that the sufferings of this present time are not worthy to be compared with the glory which shall be revealed in us. [19] For the earnest expectation of the creature waiteth for the manifestation of the sons of God.

Printed in the United States
By Bookmasters